Louis O. Coxe

THE WILDERNESS
AND OTHER POEMS

UNIVERSITY OF MINNESOTA PRESS *Minneapolis*

For E. W. C.

CONTENTS

The Wilderness AND OTHER POEMS

FLYING HOME

The plane leaps once, then strides for height;
I see the world tilt from my place,
And ordered under growing flight
The city humbled gathers grace:
O land me lucky by my love.

Now at the sea's edge beaches break
In clean return like open arms.
Ships trailing rags of wash and wake
Would charm me down had they the charms
Love lends me looking for my love.

A rounding river strives for sea
Past pleach and patchwork fields to sever
County from county, but for me
Brings salt and fresh at last together
Where lands lapse and the last is love.

For as my plane finds ground grow near
And earth and water reach her down,
My blood beats rarer than that air
And home seems where the flesh would drown.
O let me land there, laved by love.

FROM THE WINDOW DOWN

I follow from my window down
The paths my children's feet have mown
Running to the rim of bank
Where I stood once. Yarrow is rank,

Saint Johnswort straggles at the verge:
The paths like past and future merge
In a single child, myself or mine,
Poised there a season out of time.

And blown like the burrowing swallow, he
Shall next in time drop down to sea,
Dropping below my sight to find
Salt desolation. I am blind:

Another watched me so. I gaze
And see myself, a child, and raise
The head that I held so before
The bank undid me to the shore.

THE WAKING

Cold in the night the locomotive's horn
Cries over inland wastelands to the sea,
And stirring to that voice, while the house lies still
With light unspeakable rifting past the sill,
I hear a call; all that becomes of me
Startles awake, waking unseeing on a world new-born.

What dreams I start from: unreeled for private show,
Prints of the past, desires, self-repair.
Their work undone, the film stutters and stands
To this, the naked self on its own hands
And loosened to the night, this bed, this square
Of room dusted with moonlight and a stranger grown.

A horn over the water from the past:
Miles off in dark a jet of steam has blown
Vivid in air, wisped off in a warm rain,
And swells in air towards me, in seeming drowned
Where root with blossom, love with lover join,
To break in more than sound on this inhospitable coast.

I wake to withering, all my blooms at a stroke
Rotted to dust, the sound-wall broken down,
And years I traveled by the jet of dreams
Have dwindled to these bones called by my names:
All wires cut, no lens but the eye's own
Can shape the dark before me out of rage or hope.

More than a dream? Is it ghost or man who leaves
The wide bed where the other sleeper stirs?
She dreams to my motion coiling round her days,
Jostled with crowd and shades of mine she chose

5

That bloom for her, defeating miles and years.
Let her dream on forever, after shapes she loves!

I move beyond her, to night's edge and chill,
Seeing and wake at the window, and once more
The long plaint of the train warning its road
Trembles beyond my hand, desire, word.
This, then, is real? night, cold, some lost desire?
We are what we have made from chance and will,
And I lie down again in luck with her enthralled.

THE GLEN

I walked there shadowed, hearing the waters shake,
Hemmed in by hackmatack, black spruce and pine,
And crossing on moss-green stones that choked the creek
Wound up the path ascending in a line
Until the end. There, at the huge outbreak
Of root-imprisoned rock and burst confine
Of waters, came the flume dropped like a flame
Seeking outside that darkness sea to bring it home.

It took my part against the seasons' wear,
Crossing on oceans farthest from my blood
When shapes of foreign bays glimpsed once through war
Told me the heart stands fast where once it stood.
The blood returns. I took the path once more:
Loggers had lugged disaster in. The wood
Around me lay in slash, the creek had dried,
And I, accurst with memory, hid the ghost inside.

It is not waste, greed, folly that kills the heart
Or drabs the sense with foulness, but despair.
The sun bent over me. One new-sprung larch
Grew lacy and green out of the murder there
As though a promise. Man must do his part:
One to play out the curse, another spare,
A third to wait against these pass, and own
Abounding grace in promise kept and trees new-grown.

SEASCAPE: A MEMORY

This cove curved to the heart
Returning turns again;
Ebb tide rolls apart
Round rocks together lain,
Beginning from the start.

Under a granite brow
Tern, blackback and plover
Tilt as the crags allow
Away, off—recover
Delight for us then as now.

And where our lapstraked boat
Ground on diminishing stone
The rockweed thickens a coat
And dulse like rag and bone
Streams from a mooring-float.

Unmemoried neaps have sprung,
Winters have shred the pines
Yet harebells still are clung
Where the rocks wrinkle and line:
Salt embitters the tongue.

O tideless the inland waste
And waste the miles descending:
Those who turn from their coast
Lust after worlds for mending,
Their own world left and lost.

Can we turn back to find
The tide-rip still unchanged,
Ourselves clung to that mind,
Harebell and bird there ranged
With us, bent to the wind?

END OF THE ROAD

The color of October afternoon
Gave the light pause and lingered. Autumn sighed
A last and western breath. The sidelong moon
Dim in the aster sky seemed fat with tide
Growing to spring in evening, and our ride
Across the river climbing with the trees
Had stroked to silence all but the brute stride
Of engine, firing to its own decrees,
Yet underfoot, locked in and self-consumed like a disease.

We had come through in stealth along a road
That weather wrinkled. Time had stood apart
To watch the trees take back what men had owed
And lapsed in death and debt. A land too hard,
Too grudging, broke them, ending with the heart.
And we went there, smooth on our springs and tires
Past graveyards seeming laid there from the start
And holes of houses fallen, whose desires
Would darken had they stood, ringed with rugosa briers.

And autumn paused where the road had met an end
In a house grown like a grave and standing still.
I killed the rage of engine with a hand
And we set foot on earth. Time had our will,
Autumn our heart. An air stroked down the hill
And loosened leaves that flittered in the light:
The house grew darker as the gathering chill
Whitened the moon and touched the pines with night,
Biding a time, a fall with all its winter weight.

We moved. The windows gathered in the shade
But gave back nothing. We had come alone
In an emptying air, called by a world inside,
Treading unbalanced on the threshold stone
And low behind us an impending moon
That spent its light upon each wasted pane:
The year, the day and light, all we might own
Of mortal seasons failed in that dying lane,
And we turned back, our headlights sifting the night like rain.

FINITE BUT UNBOUNDED

Falselights that quaver in a bog,
Career of stars no sphere can bind:
This, of the heart brute analogue,
That, the mire of the mind.

Unstable elements, by laws
Absurd of change, move out past knowing,
Past solace. Blundering under cause,
They swallow and shift for our undoing.

We therefore fix by light long dead
On shadows and their laws of shade,
Steadying in the quiet bed
To form by man and woman made.

HERO'S WINTER

Leaf by leaf the days descend
And let the light in and the cold:
By night the widening windows fend
More black away. By morning gold
Drips softly to ground:
Oakleaf, laurel are mold.

It seems an opening out, a spell
Of vistas binding head to heart.
The eye sinks higher in a well
Of blue, now leaves have blown apart
And winds whirl with a will
In the naked yard.

Snow comes out of this, I know:
Out of the open sky comes in
Deciduous heaven. It shall throw
Deceit in white across the lawn,
Eager at sills and slow
But sure to win.

Let strip heart and house and trees—
Weather shall never find me wide.
My doors are double. Let it freeze!
I keep the fallen year inside,
Green forever with deeds
And blown with pride.

THE OLD ONES

Their passion of waiting! Then, upspringing death
Missioning green and breaking open ground
Led out the sun climbing its upward path
And brought the bride home, lived and healed her wound.

Perhaps the river, ice from bank to bank,
One day ran clear. Trees remembered shade.
All veins and powers at rumor in the dark
Crept towards a height that fell to wheel their world.

Shadow that falls here marks the land in stripes
That gave them hurt once, for their flesh was naked.
The earth heaves, turning, settling to farther sleep
And shadows fall—gallows, cross and grating.

Why should we try to feel? remember loss?
After one pain and death, they went away.
Pain was the worst, whether of fire or ice.
What quarter is the wind's? Can someone pray?

I have forgotten what the old ones knew:
Out of a fire called summer came a fall
That sealed them winter when a cracked wind blew.
They died. We live—here in what they called hell.

THE FLOOD

Castaway, an ark between two dreams—
The past and a rising future still to seek—
We live by current, move to neaps and springs
Until the bird with olive in its beak.

At stand, the waiting water of our blood,
Island, the heart. We turn on them to live
While the pole wanders and a ceiling cloud
Seals up desire—part vulture and part dove.

The world flows to a present where one rock
Grows up to cloud above it and lays down
Waters at its base. After the wreck
We close with hunger and strike out to drown.

THE MYTHMAKERS

The winter window gathers all outside,
A wideness reaching to the winter sea.
Failing in rows the sapless oaks would slide
Within a room. Salt cries from each tree
"Death of the heart" and whitens where it dried.
The rocks show blackest farthest in the lee.

This weather beckons with a thousand glances—
A dazzle of snow and sea that shatters glass,
And death shows loveliest of mortal chances
Sacred outside the window glazed in ice:
In soft unsounding fall the avalanches
Poured from the boughs seem promise to possess.

Not of this sea born, never on any shell
Of this shore naked, never rosy dame,
Flesh, Aphrodite, rippling on the swell
And on her mollusc melting hither came:
Desire of minds, wrapt in a soother spell
Than bears a goddess here, fed forth such flame.

We trap our fire in rock. Why should we lure
A goddess to a net, love out to die?
Fix us a polestar, glittered cynosure
Of ice beyond all heat, that we may lie
With essence naked, with the zero pure,
The goddess death, our petrifact of sky.

THE LOT

The lot is bitter by my father's mound,
Where my mother lies, wind has a cutting edge.
Snow lights and banks upon that burying-ground
A winter's barrow lined along the hedge;
And I have stood there under the rotten sky
Brimful at the graves where man and woman lie.

I know their will. Their house is left forever.
Bare to the walls and ceiling, stripped and sold,
The rooms rang to my step. The past aquiver
And hungry for new hearts made me its mold,
And though I locked one-half a world behind
The key I keep is master of this blood and mind.

I stood on the step and the sea wind slammed the door:
"Can you alone go back, are you that one?"
What need? I was the curse the living bore:
Now I must live their sin in me to come
And take back evil made for me by birth
With interest I compounded of their quickened earth.

What should they think of him who stands—not long—
By the arbor vitae next the iron pale?
Can they hear calling of their blood or tongue
That speaks their failure who in his turn shall fail?
Lines on the stones, snow on the raw new year:
Names and the time are done, I must look otherwhere.

LENT

Now as the flesh parts, weakened by the cold,
The season probing shivers on the bone:
Iron will enter, and the Lenten soul
Will sepulchre behind a winter stone.

Yesterday over the shoulder of a drift
A sun-shaft struck a wellspring where the wind
Blustered the driveway clear. I felt it lift
An odor from the ground. The clearing burned.

Above, a traveling vector of brave geese
Drove to the northward and I felt a yearning
Crying beyond hearing, and I cried it cease—
I, knowing ice hard at the heart of burning.

Beyond the river other gathering flights
Wild with the lying rumor in their fledge
Made ruffling stir. How could they chance those heights
As though their sense and season made a pledge?

Yet equal with the clouds that pondered snow
They struck for altitude and northern ground,
Far beyond March, beyond whole years they go
In search of promise given, lost and found.

PENTECOST

Exhausted silence, betraying like a smoke,
Fog from mismated air and water grown
Comes in a sift and mystery through oak
And clustering pine tops, leaving all alone.

At the airbase radar has homed-in the planes,
The frequencies are still and gone the pilots:
Only a rifting gull, low over pines,
Has stomach for the sky and breaking silence.

Is the river there past the slope you cannot see,
And do the black ducks puddle next the shore?
In your house are loves locked in who, to break free,
Would murder nature had they nature's power?

Under the weather-stripping seep the stains
And pool in disaffected rot like cells:
Is there no world outside? nothing remains
But separate lives inside, grown separate hells?

This is not sorrow but the naked stare
Into the empty window of desire:
The eye sees only. Hands may touch like prayer
Gone out towards love as to a living fire.

SPRING NEAR THE AIRBASE

A jet from the airbase wailing out of sight
Cuts in her afterburner, rolling time
And space out flat and level with her height,
While under the trailing sound geese start their climb,
Heavy, unheard and straggling toward their aim
As though this spring had summoned each by name.

The radar search planes bound for Newfoundland
Go over the fisherman's drag or mackerel seine:
Whether at ebb or flood, the tide shall stand
Eternal to their height, the coast of Maine
Curve out its coves, vectors of course and speed,
Pips on a scope, a fallen magnitude.

Unclouded quadrants gather to a sphere:
Weather from here to Gander, rare as glass,
Tiers in a choir of engines hunting air
And radar flinching at the touch of mass.
High beyond birds and rigid under noon,
The planes seek home unpeopled as the moon.

AMERICA TO HUNGARY, 1956

Here by this inlet where the snow comes down
And seals the world out while love keeps us warm
We let the heart pump blood as though our own,
Saying again, "We have our way with storm
And violence moving eastward out to sea:
A central heat, the order of our days
Shall keep us while this passes. Ploughs shall free
The driveway, and for this time we can praise
Disaster prisoning us within its hands,
For they must open. Nature takes no sport
In killing; time will always make amends;
We shall play God and choose to keep this fort . . ."
While on the stricken air, faint as our wills,
We hear of dying like the sea in shells.

A STUDY OF HISTORY

Warm sun, cold river, mist—
Do these make morning fresh?
To the anthropologist
Knifing under the flesh
Our Culture breeds in fog
Heavy with time gone by,
Stinking rank of the bog
And a future blind to the eye;
Yet over the sill of morning
Sun cries six o'clock,
Flood tide slack at turning
Speaks of eddy and rock,
The osprey's hover, the quiver
Of current where herring run,
Cold life in the river
And flesh warm in sun.

WATCHING BIRD

Deep in the marsh and dappled woods
I saw a thrush's staring eye:
Part of the brush and undershades,
He watched me come there like a spy.

The eye deep brown and ringed with white
Beheld me standing out of place
In shadow, seeming no way right,
Least of all, motionless a space.

He perched low on a rotten stump,
He cocked an eye and took my time:
Cones from the pines made slide and thump
From green height to the bottom slime.

Had I not moved, I still would stay
Stared out of countenance, a fool
Who looked-at shall not look away,
Foundered and covert in a pool.

DIESEL TRAIN

Pressure has trod air into heat.
The pistons falter. Like a gun
Recoiling, the convulsive beat
Stampedes combustion to a run

And the terrible thrust turned out for use
Engenders energy by change
Under ten thousand BTU's
To force no worship can assuage,

While clinging to the bridge you clench
To the flattening bellow of that lung,
The rumble in the bowels, the stench
Of oil burnt and metal wrung,

And stagger as the wave of thrust
Like madness settled to its end
Breathes generation out of dust
And seals your forehead with a brand.

ARBOR VITAE

Close by my house the trees leaf out and reach
My windows, casting seeds along the sill:
First light at morning shows them nearer grown:
The black ash lifting, white-oak, birch and beech
Press in and crowd the pines against the hill—
A darkness growing to itself unknown.

Blossom goes by, its cadence overcome
By spring unfolding in a green cascade:
Box elder, maple, aspen flickering light
Show by the poise and virtue of a limb
How deep their names lie at the heart of shade
And move the heart to know and name them right.

Now fir and feathered larch as the woods falter:
Willow grown yellow in the meadow swale
And high as cedar on its dryer ground
Gives way to groves of poplar saplings, alder
And juniper, since even trees must fail
And nameless move in consort without sound.

Uncertain masses, feeling joy nor hurt,
They grow in perfect concord without aim:
The wind that bears their seeds, forever new,
Knows none it touches. Though it touch the heart
May beckon none from darkness with a name,
Calling one laurel, another bay or yew.

READING AT NIGHT

Reading at night with fire alive and shadow
Quickening along the wall, and one bright pond
Unstirred, the book and I, I have felt follow
An ice-edge on the heat's releasing hand.

What men or images have swarmed the page
And beat my blood? Lovers a long time dead,
Tempests of minds, wind of a passing rage,
And all forgotten when the words were said.

Sorrow, desire, the heart's loved self-deceit
Dance in the cavernous mind like shapes of fire:
Why should they move on centripetal feet
To concert at the center of my sphere?

Has not life stirring grief to move a stone?
Has the world beyond my ribs worn out disguises?
Under the heat and light, for me alone,
These pages' images fill empty houses.

Surely I dream so deep I shall not tell
This warm immurement from my mother's womb,
Nor waking at false dawn to the cock of hell
Fall out to passion flagrant as my dream.

THE HOSTAGE

The rope that binds this child about
Is sorrow, winding no way out:
He stands by the hawthorn hedge, and bound
Takes in the prison of his ground.

Brothers and friends, the other side,
Pass by and leave the wounded wide:
Untrammeled they scamper out of shade:
It was for them the sun was made.

The child clings to the fence to touch
A stake, as though it bore as much,
And over his head the hawthorn thrives
In clouds of blossom cloaking knives.

In grief, however word or hand
Reach out for love, the bitter end
Snarls in a bight and shall not part
Though thorn or blossom touch the heart.

FALL OF LEAF

The sky ran down in rain all night,
This morning all the earth is brown:
Trees give up their leaves to light,
Water has brought autumn down.

Whoever rakes and burns in mounds
The leaves so scored and stained by air
Would level forests to the ground,
Make deserts of his own despair.

Some who have stunted under shade
Must hate whatever grows to die:
Indifferent heaven makes them mad
And light strikes evil in their eye.

The naked oak, last night as dense
As water with a swell of leaf,
Stands like a gravestone on their sense:
It is the monument to grief,

Grief for the husk that seeks the earth
Though soul call to a farther range,
Turned to a child, cries out on birth,
Would live forever, worships change,

Levels under final ground
The growth in vain that storms at heaven,
And through the open seasons' round
The leaves like fallen lives are driven.

AUTUMN NYMPHAL

Say no more than sober truth
When October dries the marsh,
Birds pipe single notes, and youth
Feels rotten and its weather harsh.

Do not speak of love where hollows
Fill with leaves and ruined air,
When the birches smoke and willows
Strike the posture of despair.

Touch me not. My blood like leaves
Seeks the season of the ground:
What have I to do with loves
And graces? See, the world moves round,

All's removal, time is distance,
Marsh-grass drying, failing sun:
Take your hand from me whose senses
Breed the hunter and his gun.

PEACE WITH SKYROCKETS

Can you hear this blast? Rockets or cries for peace?
The magnitude and speed streaming beyond
Old vectors leave antennae and are loose
In an evil time laid open at both ends.

Peace as the world gives, neither blest nor blessing:
What shall they say, the Savo Island dead
Who burned, by star-shells lit, or in steel casing
Took an intolerable succubus to bed?

By that humpbacked island, which burned out the life
With a rarer flash—heart's hate? or the mind
In the vicious arc of error cold as ice
While the doomed, a-stare with vision, were stoned blind?

Quincy Astoria Canberra Vincennes,
Blood-warm water of New Georgia Sound:
Can peace the world makes fit flesh to the bones
Or heal the rotten mind, drained like a wound?

The mind's a monster that the red heart feeds
And melts to its desire in the dark
Breeding new vectors, power course and speed
To weld with flesh and fire it, like an arc.

NORTHWEST WIND

Though it is May and three whistling ospreys stand
On rising air over the river cove,
Though the maples drip red beads along the ground,
This wind, stiff with the past, finds where you live.

The horn of Roland harsh as blood has wound
The passes, cries disaster at Bull Run,
A requiem at Passchendaele, over New Georgia Sound
Peace to the iron bottom and the men.

Think of those windward and seabound at their haul—
Handline, pot-warp, setting trawl or seine—
Think how this heaving wind shall find them all
Hove down, castaway or fairly home.

Cry quarter, then. Draw shallow breath and quick:
No air that passes but has brushed with death
And drawn out mourning miles and hours of arc
Touching you here with past and future both.

WINTER HEADLAND

Watch before daylight die—
Ice at its center—
Old-squaw and Golden-eye
Wearing the winter.
East from this basalt slab
Spain gazes toward you,
Nothing between but drab
Water to ward you:
Flooding beneath your feet
It calls disaster:
Salt on the stiffened cheek
Tells who is master.

Seguin the lighthouse rock
Gives vessels entry
Westward to naval dock,
Cradle and gantry.
Far to your right and left
Eastward the paths go—
Take the wind's winter heft,
Sheepscot and Casco,
Roll her Atlantic wide
And to become her,
Sluice her in southern tide
Bringing back summer.

Cloudfall and snow have full
Arch to the welkin

Save where one lightstruck gull
Burns like a beacon
Gathering wisps of day
Once now together
Lest between here and May
Light die of weather,
Blue turn to posturing,
Green, a romancer,
White, lovers' questioning
Deaf to the answer.

WOMAN AT THE WINDOW

The lights grow up in windows as day fails
And falls away from brilliance. Behind glass
A power does its office and I guess
Alone here how the blood climbs as light scales
The veins like towers, how desire coils
About the heart and in quicksilver press
Gives warmth to light, brings motion to the mass
That evening bathes in ardor and day kills.

When will my love come? Day was vacant time.
Now as the night shakes millions from its towers
And all go out to darkness, one will climb
My veins where they keep offices and powers
I fill all day with darkness to the brim
And now fling open, spilling love in showers.

THE TRAIL

Tracks in the snow that labor and are lost
In trees like headstones, pine and hemlock stand,
Have started from my door, and as the first
Prints on the past, are first to equal ground.

Into the wood, where winter without sound
Shall foil the trespasser and wind him in,
A man has gone: pointed to their end
These tracks lead out. Here where they begin

I fit my stance to prints before they fill:
Both of a size, they make a single track
From the door away. Pause here on this knoll
And see a rag-bag heaven on its back,

A house in air. Tracks that have scaled the sky
Tumble a vortex downward where the wood
Gathers the trail at last. Is that where I
Must whirl and cower with the sheeted dead?

AIDS TO NAVIGATION

Like a vessel far from shore, its own close world,
This house at morning, fathomed under fog,
Stirs to a vast stillness. Like a horn
Of a far-off cape, the diesel train gives tongue
And another day, a long swell out of time,
Lifts up again, then runs to the west unseen.

Beginning here, reluctant as the light
That speaks of stirring though the mind's for sleep,
We feel the dreams we start from leaking out
Staining the day a stiller tone and deep,
And rising can we tell which realm is real:
Of fog and stillness? of the dreaming will?

Almost outside of time, set free of space,
The heart almost persuades, "No one will care."
Looking to the window, find a face
Familiar, drowned in glass, that seems to stare
Forever inward from the other side
That backed with fog like silver has gone blind.

A jay calls flinging sound and shape like stones:
The diesel winds again, drops strike the sill,
But still the fog clasps, dreams still hold their own,
The eye looks in as though the heart had skill
To fathom seas, fix heaven with a star
As blind as mirrors; like a heart, on fire.

GROUP-DYNAMICS

What we must love is single, one at a time:
A wife, child, one particular high place
Found out from a friend, and when a name
Falls in the small heart, we can lend it ease.

No name that masters me but fell on ground
Life comes from—spare, a plot to free from lien
And fit to eternity, yet fenced around
Not to keep spoilers out but keep me in.

Why should we let in traffic and rare game
To the familiar family lot that can run wild
When the mind runs after millions and brings home
Whole albums—to find murder in its fields?

If my neighbor will, let him come in need alone:
I would not raise my house to block his view.
Our lots are cast together. One by one
We bury strangers and are raised up new.

SNOW SCULPTURE

From west to east the drifts roll blowing smoke,
Crests in the sky, hollows clear to earth.
Furrowed and worn as waves before they break
These combers tower, soft to the eye as surf.

When will they break? Listen: who hears the rote
To the eastward where all night a making wind
Has broken sea on rock? Below that weight
Of snow and water, dreamers have slept sound.

The drifts rolled over them like shoreward seas
Visions as cold and brilliant as a wave,
And rapt beneath, what should they know of ice
Who quenched their ardor in the dream they love?

Breathing and warm, they will not freeze or drown
But turn to a loved desire beyond cold.
After such sleep, the waking: one by one
The lives come out, warm from the dream they held.

BETWEEN WORLDS

"Wait for me," said spring. "I'll not be long."
  But we grow old. How long till spring be come?
  Spring said, "Winds change. See, the snow is gone
  Yet you indoors say, North and death are one."

  What should we say? As a sunburst strikes a drift
  The blue like a door slams fast again with snow.
  Is this your promise? This is our belief!
"I come as I must," said spring. "I wait for you."

  Come then—to stay! When we were young, the seasons
  Could spin like tops or tell four classic acts
  Of soul in joy, death by time or poison. . . .
"Was that your play?" said spring, "a trick of clocks!"

  A game of hearts! Winter unwinding spring,
  A fallen summer. We have run you down,
  And you must come or find your world unstrung.
"I come in hosts," said spring. "You die alone."

FOR MY SON'S BIRTHDAY

Alone at the high window of the house
Your great-grandfather built before my mother married,
I see the draggers fishing the old grounds,
Their gear new to me and their lines. All's discarded
That I knew in summer days when, like you rolling
Time and space like a hoop, I felt their flowing.

They grow beyond us till we call it change:
Rapt in pursuit, I did God knows what hurt,
And seeing now it was not I who ranged
But time and will who drove me, have I heart
To watch you range, and neither sight nor speech
Mark you even now beyond my reach?

At thirty-nine, what has my life for yours?
What sins of mine, some of them reckoned at last,
May figure forth as signs, as bolted doors
Keeping you clear of griefs like these at least?
What a man learns, what you shall learn, comes down
To Goodbye, Good luck: take nothing for your own.

Why should I hope for you against all reason,
All quiet, when our world will deal with hopes,
With all my awkward, desultory canons
Like a trap sprung, and the slave loose once in ropes
Checks viciously to nameless metal laws
And cramps down with his brothers under cause.

You will see what sorrow's here, too late for gain,
When you have years to look through of a power
Making life-size this far-off day and man
Who could see nothing of your heart, desire
And chance. Yet will you turn, reverse the glass,
That such estranging may forgive and bless?

Do what you must: the time is in your eyes.
Fear nothing the world tells you, nor my words.
Why should an old fool tell a young fool lies
Though true for him because they fed his years?
Live to yourself, God's grace and those few souls
Who know men keep a devil in their bowels.

And live in joy. Set free the dead and kill
New-foaled chimeras with a blessing eye.
When I am earth and sons of yours grow tall,
Open them windows wide enough and high
For fear of falling, givers of sky and sea,
Old ground or new, slaves to the end, but free.

THE WILDERNESS

Men in their times shape towards a visioned end:
Moving to stars, transistors, shapes of dreams
Or shuddering to three crows on the wind,
They are blessed by priests. And as a whimpering
    child
Will tug one corner of his mother's dress
Till the whole garment hangs awry, so we
Pluck for attention at the shift of truth—
Seeking no image of the world seen whole,
Only a corner lit by vision, dream,
By fire of self alight with its desire.
So with the lives of dead men and their lies:
Where motive and action, grown corrupt with time,
Tangle and litter, vision must keep clear—
Transparent bottle holding stick and string
Plaited and meaningless. Then the designer comes
And pulls his wire. And the model springs
Up straight and rigged, imperishable under glass.

◆§◆

Duclos swung the door to. The dip-flame flared
    in draft
Startling Rouville, who dropped his breviary
And smiled: "I see it's settled. Huron country?
Or . . . well, tell me." The other, square and heavy
Under the cassock, strode across the room
And kicked a beech log back into the fire.
He frowned against elation and spoke harshly:
"You would not guess . . . Listen, Rouville,
    the governor

42

And Father Becque have planned it. My first mission
Is to Acadia, to Norumbega." "When?"
"*They* know. I shall be ready for the time
 But let it be soon." Then his tone grew softer:
"I had hoped not to go alone. My guide
 Is Peter, the Huron I baptized. I hoped . . ."
"Yes. Becque and the Order do not mind our hopes,
 The work being all. My mission is the old one,
 Huron country." Silence fell. Rouville
Got up to stand beside his fellow Jesuit
And friend. He thought of Peter and the day
The outcast Huron slouched to the altar rail
And took his first communion. Rock too friable
To bear a church. "They are not only souls,
These savages, but men, too. Father Becque
Is hard. A soldier born. Pray with me now,
Now that you go. They plan a land made new
And clean for Christ, yet the savages you go to
Are not so made so soon." Duclos put out
A broad hand for Rouville to clasp: "I've prayed
To be delivered from desires of the mind,
From self. It's true. Yet how to claim the land
For God, the Order, and for France?" His question
Opened, and in the low-beamed, smoky room
The two priests felt it. Duclos, of peasant stock,
Spoke little of his heart's wish. And Rouville,
Who knew how the landless boy by force of will
Had taken up the hardest regimen,
Was bound too close to tempt intemperate speech.
He tried no answers.

                    We today look back
Over the dwindling centuries, the felled forests
And hurdled ocean now, seeing their plans
For what they were not, the men being dead

43

And rotten with baptized Hurons from the long houses.
The names they called on—France, St. Joseph, Christ—
Are names still, more or less believed in still,
And the passion of their calling has run out
Long since into the longed-for folly of their martyrdom.
The wicked country has been humbled. Iroquois,
All the Five Nations, now put out to grass,
Protestant reprieve and tourist trade.
Rouville had written early that first spring
Before the shadbush startled white in the swale:
"They come to trade, silent and sprung at the knees
And listen to mass. One cannot see their minds
Nor know what our symbols call up to their eyes.
I pray continually for their souls, believing
That they have souls." It would be difficult
For the scholar, gently bred and stocked with doctrine
To see on the shingle at the rock's foot savages
Naked and hushed and call them sons of God.
But spring flushed down the arteries of the land
Forcing the blood to bloom. France was the rock,
Quebec, the crescent tip of God's outpointing
Finger that should direct the work of saving.

The last ice trundled out to Northumberland Strait
Is gone and Montreal takes in her ships
Locked from her all winter. Now they trudge
High out of water as the slow screw dips
And sluices, bound upriver for the docks.
And the riches of the country tier the holds:
Lumber, grain, beef, butter, troops and gear
Till the plimsoll mark is at the water's edge.
Change comes with seasons, raiding the land
And taking with violent right hand while the left
        pours bounty.
Over the Gaspé and Cape Breton, the caribou barrens,

Acadian land southwest to Sable Island
It moves, the bland season. Then mauve orchises
With smell of death come out in marshy soil
Where the loggers have left slash. Sheep laurel
With pink intricate shells of blossom scentless mingles
In a sea-sloping field with pungent bay.
Cut over and dead to profit, the country stirs
To towhee and yellowthroat in the alder clumps
And God's left hand sifts life with summer fingers.

Rouville left in October for Huron country.
That day he and Duclos stood on the beach
And watched the loading, finding no parting words.
Duclos, four-square against the wind, at last
Said: "I had not thought to work without you,
Yet the Order knows its soldiers. I have prayed
Deliverance from desires of the mind
And I ask your prayers." Water and commentary
Of wind destroyed Rouville's response. The two
Clasped hands and the river sundered them. Duclos
Turned round and faced the rough climb back,
    not looking
Again to see his friend wave.

                    Beyond Acadia,
Land that drops down New Brunswick into Maine,
New England lies, a country of silent threat
Unknown and a steel edge at New France's flank.
Priests of the Order, coursing Frenchman's Bay
And down to the Penobscot, perhaps once
With Abenaki converts summering
At the Five Islands between Kennebec
And Sheepscot (where now sentinel Seguin,
The island lighthouse, groans in the fog all night),
Have seen the English, sour and prosperous men.

The savages know them. Has not their King Philip
Mitred their houses to burnt gable-ends
And harried their villages almost down to Boston?
This continent was holy. Heretic men,
Damned yet reaching out like oil on water,
Could kill the high emprise, seal off the land
From France and savage souls from Paradise.
Becque said: "The savages shall take our part.
Let the Abenaki be our weapons marshaled
Against the English. Though they die for us,
It is God who finds them worthy for the work."
The Abenaki. The stolid, sullen tribes
Scattered from Nova Scotia through New Brunswick
Into King Philip's country, Pennacook.
Becque waited for his will to take on flesh,
While the governor fumbled in his mind
Its stock of greed or piety or power.
Becque crossed the room. "We cannot wait," he said,
Opening the door. Duclos rose from the bench
And faced him. In the half-lit anteroom
They stood as outlines of opposing strengths,
Short heavy men accustomed to half-light
And solid where they stood. Becque nodded once
And turning strode in to the governor's desk
To lean on clenched hands between the candle flames.
The black shape of his curved back said "Decide."
The shadow of steady motive, the dark shape
Between two lights, was all Duclos could see,
Yet the governor could see Becque's face: "The plan
Is yours as well as Father Becque's," he said.
He worked a pen between his ringed white fingers:
"I must know more. We cannot fight the English
Alone, nor trust the savages . . ." Duclos
Stepped forward with the candlelight upon him:
"We bring them God and life eternal. Surely

When they know that, they and the land are ours
And Christ's. My life upon it. What we do
Now in the first of bringing God to them
Shall make direction. What has brought us here
But love to God and to his glory?" Becque
Was silent in saturnine darkness. Duclos moved
Bending below the candlelight. "The Abenaki.
The Abenaki shall be God's elect
To stand with Christ against the heretic
And, dying, be delivered by the Faith."

A mild November morning, drawing mist
From water. Peter's birch canoe spurts out
And into whiteness, carrying Duclos
Whose black soutane hangs in the fog alone
An instant, then removes like a black light.
Becque, a shadow left, stands on the shingle,
One arm in benediction raised to emptiness,
Having stirred the hand of empire and its God.
The Jesuit's way lies through Huron country,
Portages, hurtling flumes of the Saint John,
Saint Croix, Penobscot. The huge land
Locks itself secretly in winter as
Duclos and Peter, God supporting them,
Move on the wicked river towards Acadia.

" 'Retez. 'Coutez." Peter picked up his paddle
And laid it crosswise on the gunwales. Wind
In the balsam hushed and squalled across the water
And Peter rigid said the one word, "Mohawks."
Duclos sat stiffly, listening, hearing nothing,
Only conifers and hardwoods in the wind,
Sat listening, listening while the paddles dripped
Drops black in the sunless afternoon. "Comment . . ."
"Taisez." Peter thrust a finger up

And Duclos saw his eyes. Beyond the hither bank
A woodcock burst the thicket and he saw them
Slumping in file. His hands groped for the crucifix
As Peter's tightened on his paddle, sliding the blade
Edgewise into water. "Ils ont vu?"
"Non." They vanished, red and ochre-stained
Like late leaves into the passing softwood trees.
Mohawks were moving. Mohawk blood was up
Seeming to break surface in their paint.
Bound for the Huron towns and autumn kill,
Compelled by their blood-passion, Mohawks came.
Duclos and Peter shot for the farther bank
And hid the bark canoe under the leaves
Ochre and red still. In an instant's flash
He saw his Mohawk: a tall, lank man bent loosely
Scooping up water in a cupped right hand
But the eyes glancing blackly in swift arcs, seeing
The portionless wilderness as a lookout's ocean.
His hair, shaved off to a single black cockade
From nape to brow, stood stiff with grease like iron,
And the daubed planes of the face, red yellow
    and green,
Mocked the dear suffering of El Greco's Christ
By light and shade. The curved tense loins
    were wrapped
With hide that would be soft to touch. The left hand,
Swung back from the bent body, held a gun,
A Dutch gun with a long and blundering stock
That would batter a man's shoulder.

                    The two men
Lay hidden as night fell, the Jesuit
And trembling Christian Huron, lay thus cramped
Between the rocks in yielding tarnished moss,
Watching beyond sight. When dark was thick

Peter said, "Bon. P'vons partir." They straightened up
And shifted to the water's edge like beasts
Come out to drink by dark. The thin canoe
Looked thinner resting on the darker river
With chuckling water coursing along its sides:
Fit trope, the Jesuit thought, for what I do
And am, the frailest vessel God could cast
Yet made with purpose, with mysterious sleight,
By which God tells men He will save His world
With weakness made immortal strength through Him.
And flushed with revelation Duclos saw
At one blinding burst the huge design:
Christ on the Cross, France on this continent,
And the river welling from the country's side
Like blood, while he and Peter let its flood
Take them for souls' sakes whither Christ's heart
    might doom.

Winter within the woods is silence, silence.
If you come from the black road, having parked the car,
And cross the asphalt blown clear by the wind
And the passage of the southbound diesel trucks,
You stop and put on snowshoes at the edge
Of silence. After ten spraddled strides,
The trees, the terror, and the wendigo.
Along the trail between snow-gathering pines
You move in a stillness sifted with light drift
Quiet to unease. The squirrel's leap
Plumps down an avalanche and stops the heart.
Jay jay jay—blue-white bird and raucous call
And again the silence. Should you be alone
And circumspect, the life around you may
Allow your presence, suffer your humble passage,
While the pileated woodpecker hitching around a bole
Lays his ear to the bark to hear the inward borer,

Then flails the wood to sounding like a gong.
This is the way of urban man. This the fear
Picking the inner skin, telling old terror,
Reminding and remaining and more fierce
Than man-made evil. And because not now
Believed-in, holds the agony of unbelief.
The interlacing web-prints show awhile
Your track into the forest, but the drifting
All day and night shall sigh along those traces
Until, traceless and lost, you are alone,
Your known world gone, around you white despair.

Snow came early that winter, thick to last.
Before dawn Peter woke to the first few flakes
Stinging his face. The world was close and grey.
He sniffed the air and went to rouse Duclos.
The Jesuit would see that morning often
But only once he spoke of it, alone
Telling Rouville, later at Norumbega,
The strict events. He did not tell his vision:
"God give me words to tell how these things happened.
Peter came to my side that dawn and woke me
Pressing a hand below my ear. I knew,
Awakening to wraiths of snow whirling like dust,
A fear of wildness and my heart thumped 'Mohawks'
As Peter strapped his snowshoes on. I followed,
Swaying erect at last. He led the way then.
I would have spoken, urged a moment's pause
That we might eat, but he fled on too fast
And I could not speak. My head was light from hunger
And the cold snow sifted down my back.
Somehow I followed Peter, cherishing
France in my mind, the hearth at winter morning
Alight and the black pot slung above the flame.
The body in its weakness curses the mind

With sensual images. I could have wept.
The red blaze, the smell of seasoned burning wood,
Hurt sweetly on my sense. So rapt by vision
I stumbled over Peter, clasped a sapling,
And a clump of snow fell from the trembled branch.
He pointed and I saw. Dear Christ, in a bound
The real world overwhelmed me. The wood cleared
To a town of Huron houses bound by pales
And it was burning. In submarine snow-light
Fire and thing consumed loomed red and black,
Curiously quiet, strange as a dream remembered
In which strange faces arrogate loved names
And speech takes shape. So did the Huron town
Afire from Mohawk torches seem to hang
Between white air and earth on a white mist,
Familiar and wild as hell."

              Then as the wind
Baffling all quarters shuffled in their faces,
The hubbub of that gutting struck their ears
As a sound of playing children, doused with snow.
Duclos went forward but Peter forced him back
Into the forest's cover. Fire stood up straight
In the windless thickened air as in a lamp.
Crowds scrambled beyond the houses to a knoll
Where on a long hut stood the Cross of Christ.
Two priests stood there and blessed the savages;
Brebeuf was one, tall with his arms stretched out,
Seeming for an instant to hold back
The Mohawk fury. After the first yell
As they forced the gate the work went on in silence.
Painted like whores, evil and wrapped in skins,
They slipped like intangible shades and chopped
    or stabbed
Into knots of Hurons. Squealing cattle, pigs

With souls by God's grace, Huron men were felled
And in one spasm of clamor he heard a chopping,
A thick sound like splashed mud and saw a warrior
Wipe off his hatchet on Brebeuf's soutane,
Then turn, break for the knoll, bursting the cluster
Of suppliants and in one swinging blow
Hew down the other. "Non, non. Restez.
Mort pour nous aussi." He must have fainted
An instant. Peter forced him to the snow,
His hand peremptory. The brutal thrust
And the cold burning on his face revived him—
Revived and he saw a vision: Père Brebeuf,
His worn soutane rich red with martyr's blood
Stood up in glory on the air: "The work,
My brother. Mine is done and left to others.
Your hour is yet to come. For God and France
Resume the Order's mission, and at the end
A martyr's crown is yours. But not yet won,
Not here."

      They stood (how long he could not tell)
Within the pine grove as the town burnt out
And watched the dismal file move off, Mohawk
    and captive,
Duclos' heart ashen as the leveled houses.
Was this the price? Must God's word be made flesh
Daily to burn, bleed, stink upon the wind
And savages stay wild? His eyes took in
No more than Peter's swaying back ahead,
And the whirling world of winter afternoon
Moved by him. What would be the end? What death?
And they pressed on that day, not speaking. Peter,
With sense of wrong, of trust misplaced perhaps,
Compelled a brutal pace. Duclos stayed by him
Untiring, his body light and his brain numb.

And God was with them, for the Mohawk raiders
Had tramped to the south, perhaps towards
    Seneca country,
While their course pointed east. That afternoon
They killed a moose foundered within a drift;
Duclos ate to satiety, knowing strength
Must not be all God's care. And when he lay
Under a fir and a clearing sky that night
It seemed the land lay fair, even to the Indies fair,
For Christ and his soldiers. The figure of Brebeuf,
Vivid in thought, alone at the vista's end,
Gave promise. Father Becque had shown the way:
"God gives the Abenaki as a sword
Against the heretic English. Make it keen."
And Duclos, awake now to the work, with strength
By Christ's and martyrs' blood, saw at the end
A wilderness made Eden for the faithful,
God walking there, and at his side the holy
Army of martyrs crowned, himself being one.

"Our Lady Mother, who in sweet accord
With God did let the Holy Ghost descend
And bare for us Christ Jesus, she it was,
Virgin and lady, Mother and of our cause
Sweet pleader, she has brought men safe through evil.
The river Saint John was not the worst of it—"
Peter would wait the breakup, though Duclos
Continually urged. Yet without his skill
In flaying the birch bark, steaming the bent boughs,
They had not found a way. Duclos, admiring,
Thought much of this canoe and how they built it—
Marvelous slight shallop perfect for use.
And Peter: in the winter mornings (March
Was winter with them still) rising at first light
He fell to with his hatchet, hardly being

Entreated from the work to prayers and breakfast.
Though he would worship after his own fashion,
He would not close his eyes for prayer. God knows
If savage converts are for Him at last
Or if they live to serve. Duclos said mass
The oftener for that, meaning to keep that soul
With sacrament and Jesuit will and discipline,
Not sparing self nor wishing another spared.
By God's and by the Blessed Virgin's help they wanted
For little. Always when their strength was low,
The belly pained with fasting, they found food:
Once finding out a wintering black bear
That on a thawing day came out for sun,
Warmth having struck down in a cleft of rock
And whispered "Spring." Sometimes deadfall traps
Or a noose and a bent sapling caught them game.
The wicked cold inhospitable dark land
Sprung like a trap possessed them. Did the manitou
Peter had worshiped wink out like a star
Beclouded by the shape of a new god
Made in the image of Duclos? For Peter
Saw luck was with the black-robe now, and power.

The rivers rotted their ice and the spring fattened.

"Norumbega," Peter said, lifting his paddle
And pointing with the blade out flat while drops
Pinked the calm surface and were whirled downstream.
Ahead where on a bend the river widened,
The hither bank curved out into the river
In a peninsula, bluff-sided. Palisades
Rimmed it and desultory smoke stood up
Against the green of forest. Norumbega.
Still on the river by the right-hand bank
They paused, as Peter caught a drooping branch
And held on. Stillness hung in the spring morning,

The palisades showed hiding like a mask,
And a kingfisher rattled down the opposite shore.
Duclos felt Peter's listening and the shifting
Of his black, noticing eyes searching the air.
Silence? Nothing at all? From behind the curve
Of land before them came a shout, and then
Canoes in a cluster breaking past the point,
Leaping to paddles. They were in the sun,
The other in the shade still. Light fell on the strange
Flotilla like a passing glory. One
Among the craft urged forward of the others,
Its paddlers pumping like a clockwork toy,
And there, then—praise be to the Virgin Mother
Who heard their prayers—they saw Rouville. A priest
Erect in the vessel's waist flung up his arm.
Sudden and dear the black soutane took sunlight.
Duclos' heart filled. He looked again and saw
The upflung arm and hand held a rude cross
Of pale peeled stems. He felt his eyes grow wet.
River, banks, forest and the leaping vessels
Were turned to walking shapes the blind man knew
When Christ put holy spittle on his eyes.
"Duclos, Duclos." Rouville's voice. Duclos knew it,
Then the vessels closed. He put his hand out blindly
And felt the grasp. Within the naked heart
Of wilderness two priests of God were met,
Two soldiers of the Order, servants of France,
Friends who had died, found now in this Norumbega.

He could not speak then. Rouville took his arm
As they passed the gates. In the hot spring sun
The savage village stank of its savage leavings
To sense unused to air less pure than the forest's.
Followed by hidden eyes they crossed the square
Hard-packed like flagstones and walled in by houses,

Seeing between the bright air and the dark
Of hut doors swarms of bugs. Rouville pressed on,
Leading on past the foul torpid ghetto
To where the land spurred farthest out in water,
A lovely curving promontory, bluff
Above Penobscot. There the chapel stood,
L'église de Saint Joseph. They halted then,
Rouville checking his stride. His church. In Norumbega,
The patron saint's new chapel rose from earth
Hard-baked and dingy. Smells of the patted soil,
Of balsam and oozed sap, commingled with
A ranker flavor of the tallow dips
Smudging reluctant flame. In a thin row
They flared before an adze-hewn rail. The altar,
A plank on two squared stumps, held a gold cross
Rouville had carried with him from Quebec.
Duclos knelt down in dirt. A slant of sun
Through an air slit in the bark wall splashed in yellow
Beyond his knees. He did not see the sunlight
Nor the slow spinning of the dust motes there,
His head up, eyes closed, seeing the hot
Red tissue of his eyelids and the huge
Enfecundating darkness, breathing God.
Rouville's sweet tenor tolled the mass: "Qui tollis
Peccata mundi." In the warm dark cell
Of Joseph's chapel, in a wild continent,
Blood of the Lamb washed clean. Christ broke like bread.

That night they feasted. Peter came to them
Saying the Abenaki chiefs would honor
The black-robes, as they called the priests, with feasting
And ritual dance. Duclos would have declared
That honor to God and his servants is not paid thus
In savage rites more fitting to a demon
But for Rouville, who said: "We thank the chiefs

And all the brethren." Peter eyed them both
Perhaps alert for signs of mastery,
Of the stronger man. Yet since Duclos kept silent
He turned to go, those lingering black eyes
Containing patience, waiting for a sign
But questionless. Duclos had moved away
As Peter left the hut. Rouville turned to him
And spoke: "They found me, almost dead, last winter
And brought me here. A wandered hunting party
That stumbled upon me after dark when fire
Is seen a long way in the winter forest.
The mission to the Hurons, my first mission,
Burnt up in a Seneca raid. The town was ashes
And a few hacked bodies. I picked up a knife
That might have human blood on it. See here."
He held it out, a cross-shaped, blunted dirk
Of European make. "I took it with me.
God's hand was in the work. My mission lay
Elsewhere. They found me starving in the snow,
The Abenaki hunters, and they brought me
Here to Norumbega, to this church
That they have helped to build. Oh not from piety.
Becque and the others—they are wrong. Until
We change their hearts we cannot win their souls.
What use to preach and die, threaten and die?
They live in a special world of their own blood
We do not see or fear. Until we save them
From fear and internecine war our holy medicine
To them is virtueless. They are a dying race
Unless we show them life. Has God no care
But for their souls? They kill and spoil and kill
From habit and centerless desire, from ignorance
Of living and hope. They are a different breed.
What though we snatch some souls from hell? They die
By plague, war, inanition and improvidence,

Fated and powerless. We can show them love
And that their fate is in their hands, by God's
Best gift of freedom. Let them learn to live."
Dusk had grown thick. Outside upon the water
A loon's high trembling call rose, and the stir
Of savage trespass troubled the still dark.
"Have we the time?" Duclos said. "Heretics
Would take the land whole. If the English spread
Their evil, the whole wilderness is theirs
And lost to God and France. What profit then
To anyone but Satan? Becque knew that,
Ordering me to find the English out,
Seek out their strategems, whetting the border tribes
Against them. I have seen these heathen die
And kill, burn up like straw. It is their lot
As it is ours to save their souls for God,
Saving the land from heresy by faith.
God wills it. Abenaki men must die
Holding the heretic down, and die in Christ
And for His church. Until the land is safe,
How can we teach them wisdom? We must shatter
The English power first. Then in God's time
Death shall pass over and the land be holy."

That was the summer of broad light and late,
Salmon in shoals, deer with new furred horns.
The life of wilderness thickened. Those were the days
Duclos used for his purpose. Peter went
As always with the black-robe his magister,
Either within the outleafed trembling wood
A stride ahead, or on the river steering
With the broad stern paddle, his black eyes alight.
Then on the appointed day the fleet swept out
Into the current, bound for open ocean
And English country. The trap was set to spring.

The dark sea-running water, the close trees
And an alley of sky above assumed a world
Secret and trustless. High and alight in sun
Ospreys with incongruous whistle halt and stoop,
Then hitching their wings in, burst the river surface
And drawing up with salmon in their claws
Beat heavily for home. The bird of Christ,
Falcon of God and fisher after souls
With cross-shaped terrible claws and dulcet voice:
Birds, predators, with honey throat and grace
Of perfect motion, strike in the brown water.
Rouville, not seeking signs, still makes out love
Designing them. They are not good or evil
But natural, worth the loving. His blue eyes,
Formerly clouded in distrust, grow wide
Forgetting for a moment the design.
Duclos had won. The night of the great dance
They read Becque's letter. In the sacristy
By the smudge of dip-light, Duclos had read
   the sentence
And it was done. Outside the savage dark
Poured mystery and sound. Then the drums trembled
Shaking the beaten ground and darkness swelled
With ceremonial dance. The two white men
Looked at each other and Rouville said, "Nothing
But evil comes of evil. Yet if Becque
So orders, I obey." He rose. They went
Into the pitch-pine-flaring square, Duclos
Ahead and certain. At their coming silence
Grew out from the center of the violent night
And one by one the leaping forms were stilled.
Duclos, alone inside the ring of savages,
Spoke, his voice hard, spoke in the native tongue.
Where had he learned it? Not in the Jesuit school
Nor at Quebec. But the words fell true

And glittering in the dark. They promised blood,
Reprieve and lust to Abenaki braves
Who fought against the English. And at last
Duclos called forth an image of the future:
A paradise, a Norumbega clean
In a summer world where the long days are idle,
Rivers alive and forests thick with game,
The heaven of Abenaki saints. Then, turning,
His eyes met Peter's, fixed on the silent figure
Who, silent, was the key to speech, the key
To unlock Norumbega, letting out fury.
Peter stood still, his black eyes deep with pride,
Contempt, or nothing. He had given speech
For this and the hidden end.

Thinking of how the prayer wisps off, how wishes
And prayers are tattered by the wind of self,
Rouville sat in the waist of the big canoe,
Seeing the osprey hunch, arch in a hunting dive
And drag the salmon trailing by its guts—
Bald fisherman, killer, hunter with talons sharpened
For gripe and the killing blow. The big bird slogged
Over the pine tops, wide wings pumping air,
Lost to sight at last. The fleet moved seaward.

They camped on an island in Penobscot Bay,
A humpbacked wooded patch off the blunt coast
Ringed round with mud-flats. When the camp was made
And fires were lit, Duclos sent parties out
For deer, and others squelched out in the mud
To dig up fat sweet clams. That night they feasted.
Lonely at the utmost reach of land
And somehow helpless, Abenaki warriors
Clung round their fires. Beyond their point of light
Atlantic moved, or the dim continent

Shifting in sleep, uneasy in its posture.
And the fire leaped. The men ate, gorging themselves,
Duclos among them. When the food was gone
He rose, beckoned to Peter and stepped back to darkness.
Quiet had fallen. Stunned with glut, perhaps
In the lassitude of a long day's end repenting
Their purpose, men lay quiet on the ground
Like litter of a battlefield, picked up and dropped again
By shifting firelight. Then Duclos and Peter
Came from the trees with burdens. Rouville knew
At once and leaped up. "No," he said. Duclos
Turned to him, smiling: "Wineskins, as you see.
I made them. Strange how a peasant's boyhood chores
And knacks should find such use. And being a peasant,
I made the brew." He set his skin down carefully,
Lifting the spout. Raising his voice he spoke
In Abenaki: "Here is drink, my brothers.
Courage and warmth for all." He gave the skin
A hoist and slipped the spout into his mouth,
Tilting raw spirit in. They crowded round him
And the skin sagged circuiting the crowd until
It lay an empty hide. Rouville, alone
Spellbound and strengthless, watched the liquor burn
Along the veins and fume into the heads
Of men unknowing. Then he swayed upright
And met Duclos, who, hefting a full skin,
Bulked wide in firelight, legs spread under his robe
Firm as glacial rock. "Duclos," he said.
"It is enough." He touched the elbow raised
And looked, mildly enough. Duclos turned round
To hand the skin to Peter. Rouville checked him:
"It is enough. You have no right . . ." He stopped
As two braves hot with liquor picked him up
Setting him back beyond the ring of light
And he heard Duclos guffaw. Rouville knelt down

There in the blackness: "Let me seek Thy will,
But let Thy light descend that I may know
Thy purpose for this land, this people." Kneeling
He let familiar warmth steal in, the glow
Of God in personal discourse, while by firelight
Savages leaped and shouted, spirit possessing them.

At dawn Rouville left. Sleepless and torn with grief
He passed the night within the thickest woods
And when the first light grew behind his back
He took a small canoe and left. Dawn reddened
And fog burnt off. The sea flashed, flickered
    blue and white
As though to be admired were its purpose,
And none knew that the Jesuit was gone,
One priest alone, to paddle down the coast
Trusting some impulse, knowing his mission dead.
Duclos had waked to see the far canoe
And guessed. The personal sense of grief, of loss,
Came bitterly as he rose and walked the beach
And knelt there in the dawn. His knees pressed hard
In gravel, sunlight struck his lifted eyes.
He prayed, holding the crucifix: "Deliver me
From desires of the mind. Yet help Thou him
Who was Thy priest and is my friend. Show him
Thy purpose that he fail not. Give him certitude."
Sun cleared the hills and trembled light on water.
Duclos lurched upright, stripped and waded in
Waist deep. The icy water numbed him till
He thrashed back to the shallows and flung up
To the beach and took the quivering warmth of sun.
Then tingling life, goodness of life, flushed over him.
He thanked God then, and turned back calling Peter.

They hugged the coastline moving south to Sheepscot,
Pausing to fish, to rest, to feast again.

Duclos had tamed them. They were his. The English
Who treated Indians like slaves would know
How dear their dour restraint would cost. Duclos
Was brother to the savage tribe. Their souls
Counted, were God's. The mission gave to lives
Of little worth immortal dedication,
For they would clean the land. The Abenaki
Knew what they knew and feared the English settler,
The sour man with a passion after land
And a grinding bargain hand. His trading sloops
And land surveyors drove the native back;
His guns, blunt as his god, killed off the rebel.
Duclos came with new medicine and hope,
Hope for largess, recapture of old loss—
The fishing grounds and fertile valley land—
And he had liquor. They went thus to doom,
Hopeless, born victims. Tall Abenaki hunter
Bitter with loss, somehow displaced and feeling
The gun uncertain and the bow outmoded,
Takes hope from promise poisoned at the root.
The scouts went out by night,
Returning at dawn, their stories all the same:
Duclos saw in his mind the town unguarded,
Pennacook risen, Abenaki braves
Allied with him, sweeping the English down
To Boston, and the gutting of the city.
Squatting beside the fire he scratched out
The battle plan. The chiefs looked on like men
Who know designs fail, know that the victory goes
To new men, that no one lies down till death.
Shadow tossed by windy firelight shaped
Duclos like rock or bear. Crouching and still
And mocked with war paint, they celebrated death
Until the tide turned, wind dropped, dawn exhaled
A cold sigh from the sea. "Too late," it said.

He rose then, the Jesuit. The chiefs stood up
Sniffing the salt air, morning sea-draft piling
Into the vacuum of the empty inlet.
The men rose, fumbling with their guns, aware
Of blood, tasting its saltiness. They stood
Kicking the last firecoals. Then without command
They drifted inland into coastal pines like fog.

Weld was a village on the Kennebec,
Village of farms sea-sloping in salt fields
That danced in morning with the white and gold
Of daisies and paintbrush, tossing clumps of blue
Wild flag and harebell. Farming people, fishermen
Who slimed their boots with salt and dung alike,
The folk of Weld slept. It was Sunday morning.
The hunters mustered uneasily in the wood
And heard Duclos' last orders. Sunlight came
Inquiringly under silver-needled spruce
With warmth. They drained the last skin, and a brave,
Young, striped with paint, stepped out into the clearing
And hollered like a great horned owl. Then they ran
Whooping and crazed. One stumbled on a stump
And his musket fired. The noise was damp with morning.
A dog barked, yet a silence seemed to hold
The running warriors, seemed to hold the time
Motionless. And Duclos, who moved outside
The neutral coloration of the trees
Felt as though vision had laid hold. He saw
The houses, chimneys, molded mounds of barns
And the warriors skimming the meadow. In that passage
He almost cried out, crying to make it last,
To keep the threat, freeze all motion there.
And in one bound they reached it, the nearest house,
Bringing fire that streamed pale orange in the sunlight

And arched in the indolence of arrow-flight
To nestle in the thatch. Flame shot upright.
Duclos put his hands out. He was left alone,
The forest trembling behind his back. God's hand
Came down upon the heretic. And they ran,
Many who woke in time, ran to the trees,
To the blockhouse. Quiet splintered with musketry
That crackled along the loopholed overhang.
One rally. One dash to set that nest on fire.
One stroke. Lay by the scalps and leave the women
For this last stoop that gathers in the prey.
And at the quivering moment four tall braves
Caught up a log and ran it towards the wall
Where the studded door hid under the overhang.
The blunt butt of a pine bole, amber and beaded
With sap, moved smoothly as the running men
Bore down. Then in one clap and thrust of smoke
The whole scene hid. A case-shot burst apart,
And all ended so. They did not look behind
At the chipped log and the bodies. There were cannon
Red-eyed at the gunports, and the standing trees
Stood green with cover. The Abenaki fled
And left their dead warm near the overhang.

Importunate alive, Rouville in death
Checked their returning. They had forgotten him.
Duclos on the shore at Sheepscot saw a black shape
Tossed up like driftwood. Torn and beaten, still
It was Rouville, drowned and smashed in by surf.
Composed for burial the beaten corpse
Was protest still. They would not touch him. Only
Duclos dared, thinking of nothing, to arrange
That wet sod. He tore off the crucifix
And handed Peter Rouville's cross-shaped dirk.
They buried him there, planting a cairn of stones,

The living Jesuit praying for the dead
And for his own death. Then, with an ebbing tide,
The fleet dropped seaward, homing to Norumbega.

Duclos had led the men that morning. Since
They found Rouville he had been lost and following,
In the canoe slack as an empty wineskin.
They gave him Peter and a cranky boat
To make his own way back. The rest set out
On squally water, heading north. Duclos
Saw the departing fleet slip past the islands
And turn the headland.

                    His agony alone
Had certitude. "My God, am I forsaken?"
The long exhaling murmur of the pines
Replied "Forsaken." Water along the sides
Said "Lost," and Peter with unquenched black eyes
Slipped the broad paddle in and out eternally.
At dusk they found a cove between two cliffs.
The twisted driftwood, silver and flung like corpses,
Had maddened him with loss had not remorse
And desolation drugged him. Up the coast
Flickering yellow marked the Indian camp.
Duclos looked towards it, as to a lost fame,
He could not sleep. Trees, thick between the sky
And his mortality, left him no breath
Until he rose and staggered to the shore
Where stars, the navigator's trust, shone white
And capable. He fell down on his knees
Imbalanced with his robe too taut, and the shingle
Dinted the yielding flesh.
"How vain to trust in men, and in myself
Vainest of all. Yet must not the mission thrive,
The land be Christ's? Send me Thy light for darkness

Rings me. Let Thy will be done." He swayed
On uneven stones and felt the breath of God.
"All I had shaped has come to nothing. Nothing
Of evil have I touched but grows the worse.
The Order, France—are these too tainted? No, I only,
Desiring martyrdom, have brought high purpose low.
Yet shall I serve. Let others, worthier, cleanse
The heretic land, but let me serve Thee still
In quiet and not desiring." In the darkness
He prayed to God aloud while the flood tide fumbled
In stealth upon the stones with a climbing sound
And overhead stars in a steady fix
Stood ready to take design. And once again
The vision burst like gunflash. Père Brebeuf
In white, erect, beckoning, stood before
A cross of fire streaming across the land
And shouted "Now!" The real world wheeled,
overturned;
He saw stars hustle, trees stride into air
And cried "Not now," falling, falling face down
Into the upborne sea. Peter bent over
To pluck the cross-shaped dirk out, wet and black.

How long since the remnant flitting the woods
came home
To Norumbega, under the rampart sliding, afternoon
Light and big on the water? Men whose own doom
They had known and felt yet fought against, as men
Fight ever with odds, are killed always, and always win.
Whenever the dropping scroll of human pain
finds ending
In the agony of God's world rolled up like a shade
And the earth laid back like the lip of an unhealed
wound,

Then shall the odd come even, at the unseen
  undesiring end.
Life shall be reckoned, and death. Both made
  wisdom then.

Until the hour of truth rings up the hour of our
  earthly trust,
Life is to promise for, the double dealer, dealing hate
And taking remorse in. Live until that certain
  clinch of time
Believing spirit, trusting the heart is wise to grow
And risking all to hold a central ground, not fearing
The weight a world bears, nor the evil.
Choice still is left us. Choose as though the world
  were new
And in the heart that life which is final love.